P. Harrison

BOOK 9 NINE

ELSIE BENNETT
HILDA CAPP

COMPLETE SERIES OF SIGHT READING AND EAR TESTS

ISBN 0-88797-072-9

The Frederick Harris Music Co. Limited
529 Speers Rd., Oakville, Ont., Canada L6K 2G4
Printed in Canada

ELSIE BENNETT HILDA CAPP COMPLETE SERIES / SIGHT READING / EAR TESTS

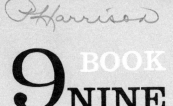

GRADE IX

PREFACE

This series of books for Sight Reading and Ear Training is designed to present to music students UNDER ONE COVER FOR EACH PROGRESSIVE GRADE these important aspects of their training.

Students are recommended to read as many of the compositions as possible from which the excerpts are taken.

INDEX

Students are urged to consult the syllabus of their choice for required tests.

O CANADA

Arranged by Elsie Bennett

is available in Concert version with parts for second piano for both Junior and Advanced players.   Price - 90c.

SIGHT READING

1. Read the music mentally before starting to play.
2. Know the key of the passage and check accidentals.
3. Establish the rhythm by counting two measures before starting to play.
4. Keep the rhythm by continuing to count.
5. Look for rhythmic patterns in scales and chords.

BEETHOVEN

MOZART

EAR TRAINING PLAY BACK PHRASES

1. Know the key.
2. Listen to the Tonic chord.
3. Listen carefully to the phrase as it is played twice.
4. Repeat the upper part.

SIGHT READING

C.P.E. BACH

Andante espressivo

BACH

Allegretto

EAR TRAINING PLAY BACK PHRASES

1. Play the upper part of the following phrases after hearing them played twice.
2. The key should be named and the Tonic chord sounded.

SIGHT READING

ECCLES

BEETHOVEN

con pedale

EAR TRAINING PLAY BACK PHRASES

1. Remember the key and listen to the Tonic chord.
2. Each phrase should be played twice.
3. Repeat the upper part.

SIGHT READING

MOZART

MOZART

EAR TRAINING PLAY BACK PHRASES

1. It is important to know the key and to listen to the Tonic chord.
2. Listen carefully to the upper part as the phrase is played twice.

SIGHT READING

1. Key?   2. Time?   3. Tempo?

KUHLAU

E. B.

F.H.5031

CADENCES

1. PERFECT or AUTHENTIC CADENCES: The chord progression is DOMINANT to TONIC. Listen to the movement of the notes in the Bass as they RISE a FOURTH (V to I), or FALL a FIFTH (V to I).
2. IMPERFECT CADENCES: The chord progression is TONIC to DOMINANT, the opposite to the Perfect Cadence.
3. PLAGAL CADENCES: Here the progression is SUBDOMINANT to TONIC. The notes in the Bass will FALL a FOURTH (IV to I), or RISE a FIFTH (IV to I).
4. It is essential to listen to the Bass.

1. Identify as PERFECT (V to I), IMPERFECT (I to V) or PLAGAL (IV to I) the following Cadences after the Tonic chord has been sounded and each test played twice.

SIGHT READING

E. B.

HAYDN

CADENCES

1. Identify the following cadences as Perfect, Imperfect, or Plagal.
2. The Tonic chord should be sounded and each test played twice.

SIGHT READING

MOZART

C. L.

CADENCES

1. How many Perfect (...), Plagal (...) or Imperfect (...) Cadences are there in these tests?

SIGHT READING

HAYDN

15

CHOPIN

16

CADENCES

1. Identify the cadences in the following phrases as Perfect (V to I), Imperfect (I to V) or Plagal (IV to I).

SIGHT READING

BLOW

MOZART

SIGHT READING MELODIES FOR TESTS IN RHYTHM

1. Clap or tap the following melodies.
2. Always count.
3. Play or sing each test while beating time.

SIGHT READING

1. Time?   2. Rhythm?   3. Mood?

KUHLAU

MOZART

F.H.5031

SIGHT READING MELODIES FOR TESTS IN RHYTHM

1. Clap or tap the following melodies while counting and beating the time.

SIGHT READING

GRIEG

BEETHOVEN

SIGHT READING MELODIES FOR TESTS IN RHYTHM

1. Clap or tap the following melodies.
2. Always count.
3. While beating time play or sing each test.

SIGHT READING

LISZT

SIGHT READING MELODIES FOR SINGERS

1. Sing the following melodies while beating time.

SIGHT READING

BEETHOVEN

BACH

SIGHT READING MELODIES FOR SINGERS

1. These tests are designed for one part to be sung while the other is played.
2. They also may be used for additional Play Back Melodies.

SIGHT READING

MOZART

HAYDN

BACH

ASCENDING INTERVALS

By repeated practice learn to identify intervals. Help yourself by memorizing the first intervals of your favourite songs, or think in Tonic Solfa, or of the degrees of the scale.

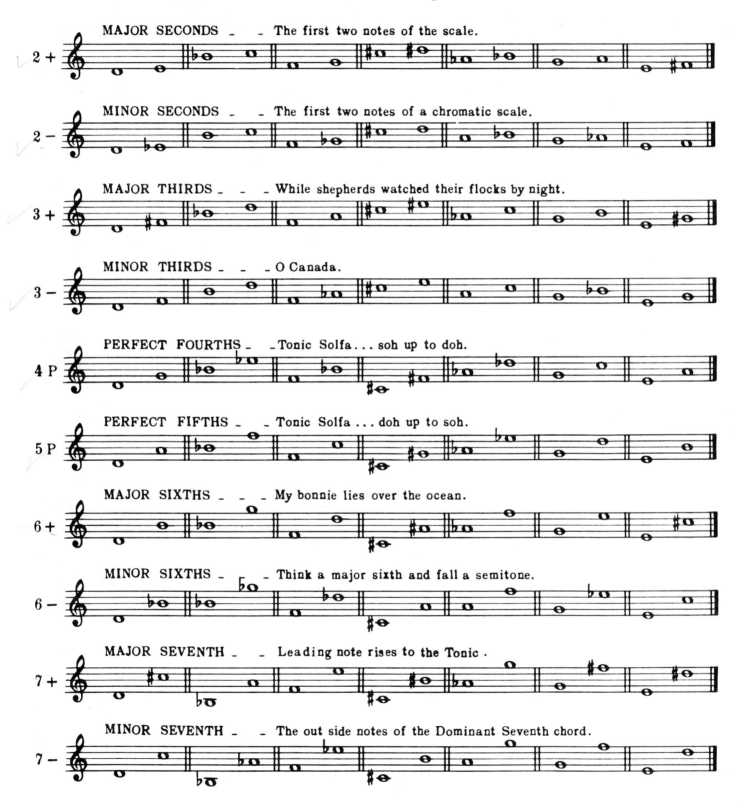

MAJOR SECONDS _ _ The first two notes of the scale.

MINOR SECONDS _ _ The first two notes of a chromatic scale.

MAJOR THIRDS _ _ _ While shepherds watched their flocks by night.

MINOR THIRDS _ _ _ O Canada.

PERFECT FOURTHS _ _Tonic Solfa... soh up to doh.

PERFECT FIFTHS _ _ Tonic Solfa... doh up to soh.

MAJOR SIXTHS _ _ _ My bonnie lies over the ocean.

MINOR SIXTHS _ _ _ Think a major sixth and fall a semitone.

MAJOR SEVENTH _ _ Leading note rises to the Tonic.

MINOR SEVENTH _ _ The out side notes of the Dominant Seventh chord.

SIGHT READING

Andante cantabile

VENTO

29

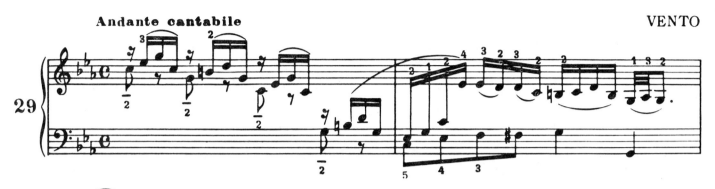

Minuet

KUHLAU

30

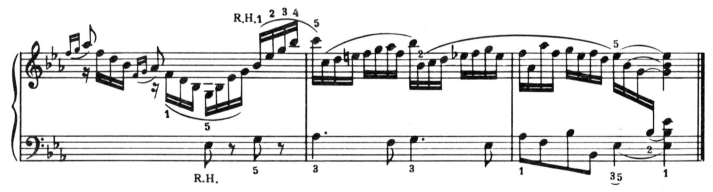

ASCENDING AND DESCENDING INTERVALS

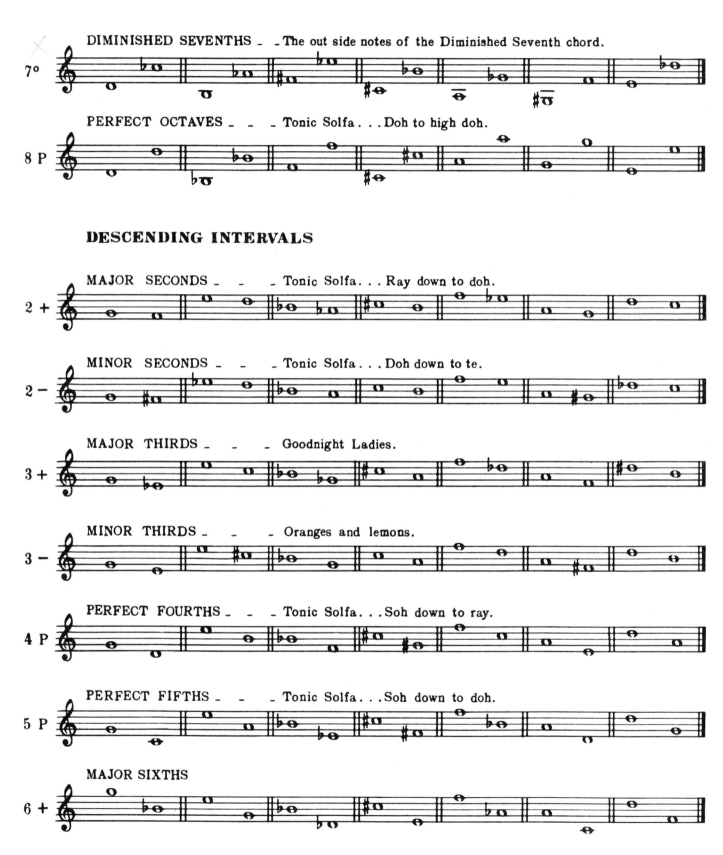

DIMINISHED SEVENTHS _ _ The out side notes of the Diminished Seventh chord.

PERFECT OCTAVES _ _ _ Tonic Solfa...Doh to high doh.

DESCENDING INTERVALS

MAJOR SECONDS _ _ Tonic Solfa...Ray down to doh.

MINOR SECONDS _ _ Tonic Solfa...Doh down to te.

MAJOR THIRDS _ _ _ Goodnight Ladies.

MINOR THIRDS _ _ _ Oranges and lemons.

PERFECT FOURTHS _ _ Tonic Solfa...Soh down to ray.

PERFECT FIFTHS _ _ _ Tonic Solfa...Soh down to doh.

MAJOR SIXTHS

SIGHT READING

Allegretto

MOZART

MENDELSSOHN

With feeling

IDENTIFICATION OF CHORDS

MAJOR CHORDS with INVERSIONS

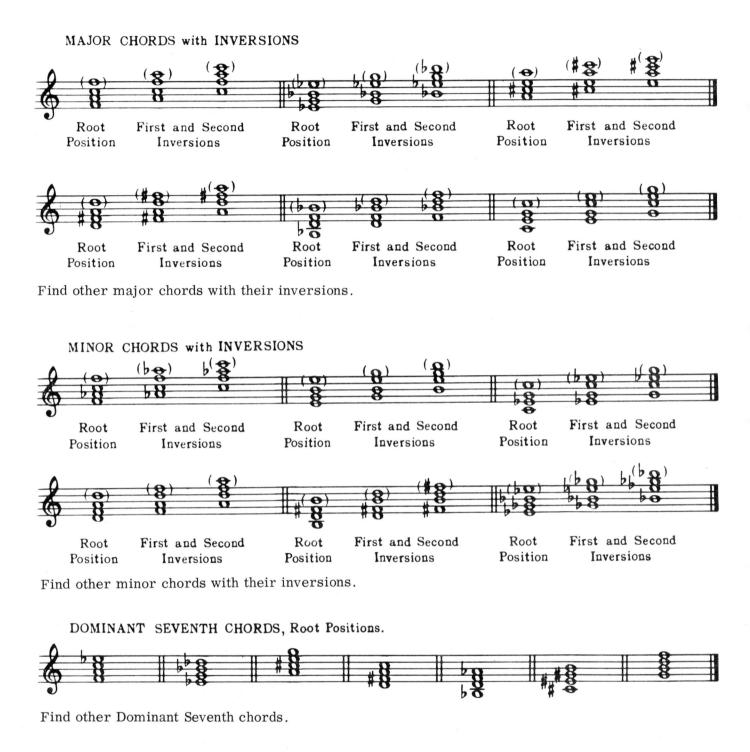

Root Position   First and Second Inversions   Root Position   First and Second Inversions   Root Position   First and Second Inversions

Root Position   First and Second Inversions   Root Position   First and Second Inversions   Root Position   First and Second Inversions

Find other major chords with their inversions.

MINOR CHORDS with INVERSIONS

Root Position   First and Second Inversions   Root Position   First and Second Inversions   Root Position   First and Second Inversions

Root Position   First and Second Inversions   Root Position   First and Second Inversions   Root Position   First and Second Inversions

Find other minor chords with their inversions.

DOMINANT SEVENTH CHORDS, Root Positions.

Find other Dominant Seventh chords.

DIMINISHED SEVENTH CHORDS, Root Positions.

Find other Diminished Seventh chords.

SIGHT READING

HAYDN

MOZART

EAR TESTS FOR MUSIC OF TO-DAY

1. After hearing each chord played twice state whether the harmony is in thirds, or built on fourths and fifths.

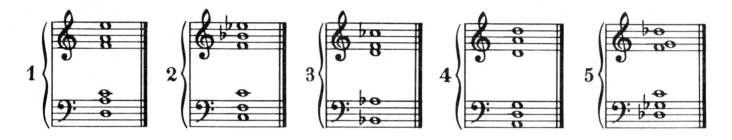

2. After hearing the passage played twice state whether the rhythm is additive or divisive.

3. After hearing the tone row played three times state whether the fourth enunciation is an inversion, a retrograde, or a retrograde-inversion.

SIGHT READING

CLEMENTI

MOZART

F.H.5031

SIGHT READING

Allegro   CLEMENTI

37

Allegretto   CUI

38

Moderato e molto legato   SCHUMANN

39

MOZART

SIGHT READING

SCHUMANN

GRIEG